Dear younger me

April Griffith

BookLeaf
Publishing

India | USA | UK

Presentation by *BookLeaf Publishing*

Web: www.bookleafpub.com

E-mail: info@bookleafpub.com

ISBN: 9789363310445

First edition 2024

ACKNOWLEDGEMENT

All glory be to god,my father watching from
heaven.

PREFACE

Words are powerful Amy's I hope you find peace
and love as you read through a collection of
mine.

In Jesus name

It's a new day
There's so much to see...to do
But first I'll pray
I don't wanna do this my way
Though you knew that already
My heart is open,I'm ready
To see you..to feel you..to hear your voice as
Yes, I did that fateful day. You will never let me
down the path, so I was not supposed to travel so
I live this life with my eyes locked in on the
castle I wanna be still
in your arms for that's where I heal.
I lift a song of thanks to you forever in Jesus
name,I am no longer the same.

Hurt people continue to hurt people

Do you hear what you say?
what is it that causes you to destroys others this
way?
the words you sling,
 with such malice sting,
and I don't think you care how they cut me
down, make me cry,all alone
I wouldn't dare make another feel so low...
like they aren't important,
 that's what your words show...
The worst are the ones that destroy for their love
of power whose words cut like swords
Do you even notice? The things you do have
only evil motives… When will you open your
eyes to the pain you cause they hate you and still
you disobey God's and the world's laws,
so why do you think you can start to heal
please don't get mad
I'm keeping it real
and it makes me sad watching the whole ordeal.

Dadu

Lie, all you do is lie
I jump from the moving vehicle before you
know it years go by I realize how far I ran from
God, from truth,
from anything that reminded me of you.
I resented you, I resented truth..
I resented God, I was like the crazed standing in
the storm holding the lightning rod. I'm going
back to you hold on my Bible… Feeling revival
 like a little girl again
Running home, saying Dad look what God did!
I was running, losing, hiding, abusing
Forgetting that Dad, you were only human, as
am I
So for me and my future, I'll keep my gaze
focused on high.
Gods found me, I am redeemed
now I look around and just want to scream!!
 Good morning
Wake up,I just wanna tell off this amazing trust

Rape

Rape
now that's a word we all hate
Child molestation has become way too common
in recent generations…
 I was one of those children who was touched,
and told it was a game, so I'd keep it hidden
I remember the shame, when I first told what
I've been done to me, it caused a divide in my
family..
When he got away with it in court, it told me
what happened to me, was in short,unimportant
I grew up, hating me, and soon started acting out
sexually. Then I was a whore, but nobody wants
to talk about the abuse from before. So my body
counts high,
I won't lie I just wanted to explain from the little
broken girl, exactly why…
I have healed, but it wasn't until my lips were
unsealed. Rape doesn't have to be shame.
Remember out of everyone you and I were the
least to blame.

Twirl girl

You are my one thing
Your blessings I receive
My hands I raise,the only thing I say is praise for
all my days
I don't care they can call me crazy,
You choose me,it's me you see
I'm scared of rejection for no reason you have
stood through every season.
Every tear I shed,you have been there waiting to
remind me what you said.
"Come to me my girl.. Let me be your whole
world.
You feel unworthy
Like I don't choose you for my glory.
It's all you ever do,stand by and wait for me to
run to you."I hear it lord,like an ancient chord
Saying it's OK April you always will be my
favorite girl. Go ahead sweetheart swing and
twirl.

Stop denying

No pain, no gain
that's what they're always saying,
But I'm tired of praying for better days, why
can't things just go ahead and change.
I've never chosen to stay and try,
it's easier to run so I'd end up saying goodbye.
The feelings you think are irrelevant
Are really so very important. It feels as though
Nobody cares with my heart tears.
They laugh and stare and tell me I'm getting
nowhere.
Positivity is barely a possibility, surrounded by
negativity
I'm losing my sanity
I'm Craving clarity, you know honesty that's rare
quality. They see a smile and don't think I have
my storm cloud, they are in denial, see denial is
bliss, and acknowledgment of the problem
means they do exist. If you weren't in denial
then how could you look me in my face and tell
me my life is going to waste. I called denial
because you say you love me, but that sounds
like hate
I just had to share….
 the way you make me feel

stop hurting me if you care
And help me heal,cause the past has been
traumatic,I don't know how to deal with the
whole ordeal.

Beautiful soul

A beautiful soul, that is the goal.
For others to see
 only light inside of me.
Who never hurts,doesn't lie and never deserts.
Who picks up when you call, helps you when
you fall down and never lets you leave without
feeling loved by me.
A beautiful soul is beauty inside, not out, let me
explain what that's all about. It's saying, even
when it's easier to go is loving others more than
you'll ever know it's listening to the hurting. It's
helpful and reassuring, hurts if it hurt somebody
else cares about others more than themselves. A
beautiful soul doesn't say it's too hard when life
gets bad they don't used to discard the joy that
they once knew,
they just push on through.
I'm not saying, I'll never be sad, or never
respond with spite when mad…
But I will strive for peace, and hopefully one
day at a time that beauty inside will start to
increase.

Dirt

Who told you that you were not enough?
That you are ugly,weak, or maybe too fat.
I bet it was someone you love…
And soon enough you feel that they weren't
opinions rather a fact.…..
See the more we care; the more their words sting
They say that they truly care
And then destroy our self esteems.
I had a tendency to say
"Who cares what they think..
Then I usually would go buy a drink or pop a
pill to try to fill a void that was so hard to heal
Then I heard a voice whisper inside
"Those statements were lies, don't forget how
the enemy despises when a chosen one rises."
Now the words do still hurt,
but I had to get up…
Get up out of that dirt!!!

Better not bitter

I bet this sounds oh so familiar to you
When you say "I got a problem"
And someone responds "I know what you you
should do!!!"
In fact they probably have a book... or two
and they usually contain some amount of truth.
I'm not saying they're wrong..
but consider this won't you?
Where do you think that help comes from…who
told them?
Come on listen really listen to what I'm saying
to you.
The things the lord gives he can take away. So as
you cry out for mercy
Remember the choices you continue to make…
Please don't be bitter
Be a better mother, friend, daughter and sister.
Then maybe your trouble will cease, just know
one way or another you WILL eventually hit
your knees.

Lean on me

Lean on me
When you're not strong
Come on I know you wanna sing
everytime you hear that song
But in our everyday existence
Is this what we tend to experience
Do you gladly help others
Or do you mainly care about yourself
If your neighbor was in need
would you answer their desperate plea
Or if I needed a friend
would you listen or turn me away instead
True compassion is what Bill Withers tried to
spread
Unfortunately I think most people just liked his
flow instead
So next time you hear that song
remember it's purpose..
We're all supposed to get along
And be each others resources.

Shame

Shame...Oh shit hide your face
Nobody would understand
Your situation was a one in a million case
Fear.. that's one you know well
Of abandonment...... or disgrace
so you create your own personal hell
Yet silly human did you forget
Jesus and what he did for me AND you??
The beatings, the cross or the stone rolled away..
Apparently if you tend to say
"I'm too far gone"
I'm pleased to remind you that you're wrong
Unconditional love to all who will receive.
That my friend is what I know and believe

Mom

Hey mom look at us
Remember us...back about nine months ago
Strung out on drugs, lacking hope
Not even connecting
My spirits rejecting
Then we surrendered our lives to him
Asked forgiveness of all our sins
Now look at our present day reality
 Jesus set us free
We now have serenity
Chains are still breaking
We won't stop praying
We're not alone
He sis on his throne and when we showed up he
said my girls are home!

Grace

Grace
What does it mean?
That I can show my face
Without fear of the unseen
The lord of lords and King of Kings
Came and cleared my slate for me
I've stayed far away
I'd use drugs to escape the pain
I've hurt other people before
But he came and my life he'd restore
Grace surrounds my life
I used to cut but I threw down my knife
To my knees I fall
Praise the lord
Now I'm going to war y'all
The enemy has no place
Don't mistake it, it's not pride
It's just Gods grace

Younger me

If I were her to meet younger me
I'd tell her spread your wings be free
These hurts you are going through daily
We'll make sense one day
Even writing this has my hands shaking
I'd tell her this too shall pass
Oh baby girl you'll grow up so fast
Everytime you start to cry
Lift your head up princess
Look at the sky
See how the birds soar
I'll be your witness
One day you'll see purpose in the pain
And sweetheart you'll always be the girl singing
in the rain
I love you I do...if only you knew all I've seen is
true.
Do you girl god will see us through

True

What makes a statement qualify as true
Is it one way or another or does it
Change from me to you
What I say is true, is to me, but would it still be
true if you were the one in that reality?
Why do I perceive things the way others do
not...
Is it the way my brains wired.. or how I was
taught?
See one thing I despise is someone who tries to
coerce me with lies and when addressed they
deny or start to cry
Like it's easier to say a falsity rather than accept
their reality, when in all actuality
It seems like insanity, how come I can't trust
family
Those that are closets to my soul are the ones
who leave the biggest hole. Cuz when we can't
honestly communicate,
Then we'll never really be able to relate
It's not possible to trust, when it's plausible the
truth was hushed
If you can't admit to me
Please don't deny it, the truth sets you free

If you choose to lie just know the evidence will
prove
Not only did you lie to me, you chose to lie to
you.

Addicts

I'll never do the things my mom did
I will never be an addict
I repeated in my head
Those words haunt me, because I too decided to
try methaphetimine
the first time I hit high
I said it's cuz I wanted to know why
Why this drug was her priority
Why she chose it over being with me
That's what I told my heart
I really thought I could choose to stop if I chose
to start
Like I was immune to the power meth has on
everyone else
You heard that right I lied to myself
Soon I was using more than I wanna admit
I was exactly what I'd said I'd never be
I was an addict
The same as my mother
Cycles repeat I've come to discover
I wish I'd never taken that first hit
I'm playing with you please
Don't ever try that shit

Cutter

Nobody understands,I tell myself
As blood runs down my hand
The blade has numbed my inner pain
Note to Google how to remove a blood stain
I know I know
Not to let it show, they'll freak out and I'll have
to go
Back to the place where I'll be held at least three
days
With others who cut, or who refuse to eat, they
hold us in a literal cage.
I'll be told I know how to cope, told not to give
up hope
Another pill and I'll be able to deal with the
sadness I feel
My depression is real
I miss school each time
The days I missed made me so behind
When I added them up
I realize how much cutting affected me
That suicidal tendency, almost got the best of me
So when you see my scars
Know being here today is a personal victory
Don't be afraid to all about my testimony

Drinking and driving

You walk in the store your friends wait outside.
Walk down the aisle hands by your side You
walk to the fridge and pick me up
Head to the counter trying to act tough.
 As you put me on the counter your hands start
to shake.
clerk asks for identification so you show him a
fake.
You rush to the car and start it up.
 I'm sober you think…I didn't have very much.
Then you drive down the road and your head
starts to sway you dont even notice the truck
coming the other way. You hit the road with a
bang,suddenly your in treachorous pain.
when u walked in that store you shoulda thought
twice
for my name is alchol and I just cost you your
life.

www.ingramcontent.com/pod-product-compliance
Lightning Source LLC
LaVergne TN
LVHW021358200726
843509LV00014B/2909